DISCOVER

Water

by Barbara Brannon

Table of Contents

Introduction

Water is in three forms. Water is in many places.

1 — Water is a solid.

2 — Water is a liquid.

3 — Water is a gas.

gas

ice

liquid

rain

solid

water

▲ Water is on Earth.

See the Glossary on page 22.

What Are the Forms of Water?

Water is a **solid**. **Ice** is a solid.

▲ Ice is a solid.

▲ Ice is a solid.

Water is a **liquid**. **Rain** is a liquid.

▲ Rain is a liquid.

It's A Fact

Clouds are small drops of water.

Water is a **gas**. Water vapor is a gas.

▲ Water vapor is a gas.

Where Is Water?

Water is in a glacier.

It's A Fact
About $\frac{1}{10}$ of Earth is glaciers.

▲ A glacier is a solid.

8

Water is in an ocean.

▲ Ocean water is a liquid.

Water is in a sea.

United States

Atlantic Ocean

Caribbean Sea

▲ Sea water is a liquid.

Water is in a lake.

▲ A lake is liquid water.

Water is in a river.

▲ A river is liquid water.

Water is in a pond.

▲ A pond is liquid water.

Water is in a stream.

▲ A stream is liquid water.

Water vapor is in the air.

▲ Water vapor is a gas.

How Do We Use Water?

We use water to drink.

▲ We drink water.

We use water to cook.

▲ We cook with water.

We use water to bathe.

▲ We bathe with water.

We use water to clean.

▲ We clean with water.

We use water to swim.

▲ We swim in water.

Conclusion

Water is in three different forms.

1 Water is a solid.

2 Water is a liquid.

3 Water is a gas.

Water is in many places.

▲ Water is on Earth.

Concept Map

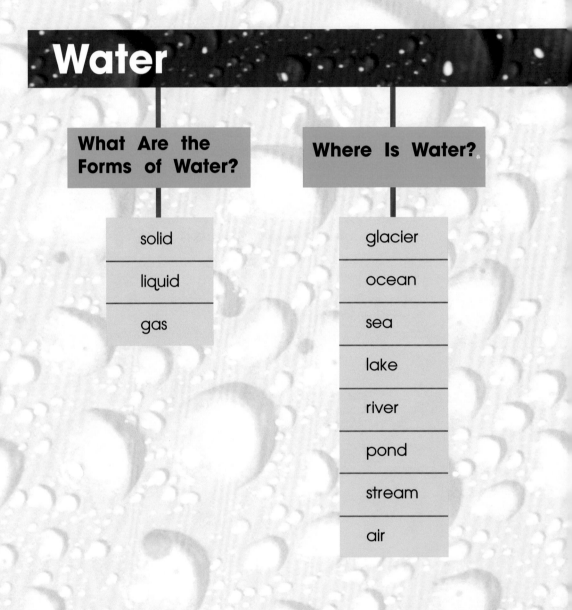

Water

What Are the Forms of Water?

solid

liquid

gas

Where Is Water?

glacier

ocean

sea

lake

river

pond

stream

air

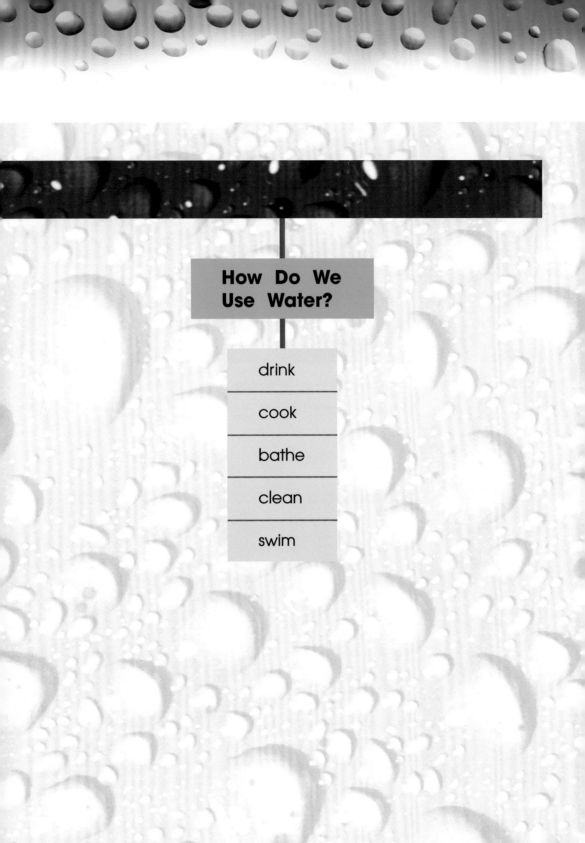

How Do We Use Water?

- drink
- cook
- bathe
- clean
- swim

Glossary

gas matter that has no shape

*Water is a **gas**.*

ice water that is frozen

Ice is a solid.

liquid matter that can flow

*Water is a **liquid**.*

rain drops of water from the sky

Rain is a liquid.

solid matter that has shape

A glacier is a ***solid***.

water a liquid that we need to live

Water is in three forms.

Index